The
DOG LOVER'S
Digest

THE DOG LOVER'S DIGEST

First published in 2011 as The Dog Lover's Companion

This edition copyright © Vicky Barkes, 2013

Cover and title page by Hannah George

Illustrations by Kath Walker

All rights reserved.

Vicky Barkes asserts her right to be identified as the author of this work in accordance with sections 77 and 78 of the Copyright, Designs and Patents Act 1988.

Summersdale Publishers Ltd
46 West Street
Chichester
West Sussex
PO19 1RP
UK

www.summersdale.com

Printed and bound in the Czech Republic

ISBN: 978-1-84953-425-3

Substantial discounts on bulk quantities of Summersdale books are available to corporations, professional associations and other organisations. For details contact Nicky Douglas by telephone: +44 (0) 1243 756902, fax: +44 (0) 1243 786300 or email: nicky@summersdale.com.

The
DOG LOVER'S
Digest

Vicky Barkes

summersdale

For Lottie the family dog, Fudge the radio dog, Milly the publishing dog, Elvis the artist dog, Rosie the babysitting dog, Phizzy the creative dog, Harvey the driving-and-jiving dog, Stumpy the seaside dog, Gus and Billy the Floridian dogs and Alfie the pub dog.

And in loving memory of Sally and Panda, the two greatest picnic raiders on the South Coast.

Contents

Introduction

*Dogs are our link to paradise.
They don't know evil or
jealousy or discontent.*

Milan Kundera

From feral beast to man's best friend, the domesticated wolf has been the object of human affection for centuries. As a well-loved pet, as a key member of the workforce or as vital support for those who depend on them for practical assistance in daily life, the dog is quite simply the most popular animal on the planet.

Featured in literature, film and television and even in advertising, they also play a crucial part in defending the country and in medical science, their brilliant noses detecting potentially lethal devices and tumours as easily as they might sniff out a butcher's window in a bustling high street.

But it is for their company that we most appreciate dogs. Their loyalty, intelligence, affection and generosity of spirit, coupled with their sheer enthusiasm for life, makes them the very best of animal companions; through good times and bad a dog will remain a reassuring constant, wagging a merry tail to acknowledge your joys and providing a sympathetic furry neck into which to shed your tears.

Demanding little in return beyond food, love, walks and perhaps a ball to fetch, the rewards of dog ownership are rich. As the American comedienne and actress Gilda Radner observed: 'I think dogs are the most amazing creatures; they give unconditional love. For me they are the role model for being alive.'

This book is a celebration of canine role models everywhere. I hope that you enjoy it as much as a particularly good walk with your dog.

Vicky Barkes
March 2011

*No one can fully understand
the meaning of love unless
he's owned a dog.*

Gene Hill

Leader of the Pack: From Wolf to Family Pet

A mountain with a wolf on it stands a little bit higher.

Russian proverb

After many years of debate scientists are now generally in agreement that dogs are directly descended from *Canis lupus* or, as it is more commonly known, the grey wolf. But while there is some evidence to suggest that dogs may have been domesticated as far back as 31,000 years ago, as to exactly when, or indeed why, dogs were tamed by man remains something of a mystery.

Researchers now believe that there are key reasons for dogs connecting with humans: firstly, dogs have become attuned to the behaviour of humans and domesticated by man over a period of many years; secondly, being bred for specific tasks, including herding and assisting people with disabilities, has given dogs a more in-depth understanding of the human psyche.

Ancient History or Shaggy Dog Story?

One of the oldest stories in the world involves a wolf, the dog's ancestor.

According to Roman mythology, the founders of Rome were Romulus and Remus. The story tells how the twin babies, supposedly sons of the god Mars and the priestess Rhea Silvia, were raised by a she-wolf.

It starts with their grandfather Numitor, who was king of the ancient city of Alba Longa, until he was deposed by his brother, Amulius. Numitor's daughter, Rhea Silvia, was made a vestal virgin by Amulius, meaning that she was given elevated status: priestess of the goddess Vesta. Now, of course, a vestal virgin getting fruity with a fella is simply not on, but when Mars came along, looking all butch and hunky and giving her the glad eye, Rhea threw off her toga and abandoned herself to his lusty ministrations. Nine months later out popped the two bouncing baby boys.

Worried that the lads might grow up and pinch the throne from him, sneaky Amulius had them thrown into the River Tiber. But thanks to a freak tide the boys survived, and they washed up, feeling somewhat dazed and confused, on shore where they were found by a she-wolf. While you might have expected Mrs Wolf to lick her lips in anticipation of a hearty dinner, the maternally inclined beast chose to ignore nature in favour of nurture and she suckled the babes instead. Later found by a shepherd who brought them home to be raised by himself and his wife, Romulus and Remus grew into fine, strapping chaps.

As adults the twins would have revenge, and off they went to kill Amulius. This done, they reinstated Grandpa Numitor as king of Alba Longa, then decided they would found a town of their own. Choosing the place where the she-wolf had nursed them, Romulus began to build walls on the Palatine Hill. But Remus laughed at his efforts, saying that the walls were so low that he could easily jump over them. Highly irritated by his brother's jibes, Romulus promptly killed him, before continuing to build his new city. Rather egotistically he named it Roma, after himself.

> ### *I love my dog because...*
>
> I don't have to get the Hoover out following kids' mealtimes!

Dogs by Numbers

- Two dogs survived the sinking of the *Titanic*.

- The expression 'three-dog night' originated with the Eskimos. It signifies a particularly cold night, when you need to snuggle down with three dogs to stay cosy.

- The song 'How Much is that Doggie in the Window?', sung by Lita Roza, entered the charts in March 1953 at   number nine. It spent 11 weeks in the charts, reaching number one in April.

- In 2006 it was estimated that in the UK there were 10.5 million dogs with owners.

- It is estimated that around one million dogs in the USA have been named the primary beneficiary in their owner's will.

Mooning About

When a dog howls at the moon, it is acting on the most basic of canine instincts and attempting to call the pack together.

Perhaps it was some celestial link with the winter night skies
that prompted the wolf to lay his song on the icy air.
For the native people who lived with the wolves,
and the wolves once ranged from the Arctic to the subtropics,
there was much to learn from them.
Is it any wonder that the myths of many tribes characterise the wolves
not as killers but as teachers?

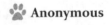 **Anonymous**

Pedigree
Peculiarities

They usually bark when there is a stranger about, but it is an expression of unmitigated joy.

Norman Strung on how Labradors
are lousy watchdogs

There are many different breeds of dog – as many as 800 recognised distinct breeds worldwide – and each breed has its own distinguishing characteristics. A description of the traits and features of every breed is laid down by organisations such as the Kennel Club, including so-called 'designer' dogs, like the 'puggle', which is a cross between a pug and a beagle.

Opting for a pedigree certainly makes choosing a dog easier in many ways, especially if you are buying a puppy; because pedigrees have a history, you can easily research the particulars and peculiarities of your favourite breed. This is, of course, far trickier with a mutt, where you may not know for sure what breeds it is crossed with. But with a pedigree pup, temperament, ailments it might be prone to, how active it is – all these factors and more besides can be fully explored before you make that special addition to your household.

Pick of the Pups

Choosing the breed that is right for you, your family and your lifestyle is as important for the dog as it is for you. If you know that you need a dog that can cope with lots of noise and a lively family, for instance, you should consider breeds such as golden retriever, Labrador or Irish setter, while the pug or the Sussex spaniel are amongst the breeds best suited to novice dog owners. If you are yearning for a walking companion then a traditional working dog, such as a collie, might be best for you, while those who want companionship without too much physical effort involved should allow themselves to be steered towards bulldogs, borzois and, strangely, greyhounds. Although traditionally racing dogs, greyhounds love nothing better than curling up for a nap, ideally in a cosy basket. 'Handbag' dogs don't, of course, generally need as much exercise as larger breeds, but you do then have to carry them if they get tired, so they're not always the lazy option; carry even a small dog for any distance and you'll soon feel like you've been pumping iron in the gym.

Before you become a dog owner, make a list of all the factors that need considering, including, crucially, how much time you will be able to spend at home with your dog, and how much time you will have to walk it each day. Read up on different breeds and make your choice based on the realities of your day-to-day life. Don't, no matter how tempting it may be, allow yourself to be seduced by the breed that you find most aesthetically pleasing.

Did You Know That...

- A tax collector, Louis Dobermann, first bred the Dobermann pinscher. It is rumoured that he created this butch dog as a means of protecting himself against angry taxpayers who sometimes needed to be persuaded to pay up.

- Labrador retriever is the favourite breed of dog in the USA, Canada and the UK.

- Hailing from Scotland in the 1860s, where Sir Dudley Majoribanks mated a yellow retriever with a Tweed water spaniel, the golden retriever grows to an average height of 23 inches.

- The greyhound is the world's fastest dog, with a top speed of up to 45 mph.

- The Jack Russell terrier is an excellent watchdog as he has a bark that is disproportionately loud compared with his miniature stature.

- According to legend, the Pekinese, one of the oldest breeds in the world, was created as the result of a liaison between a lion and a monkey. The breed was considered sacred by emperors.

DOG TALES

Boomer's human, Jo, recalls a walk on which her
'chocolate box' Yorkie proved that not all of
his breed are prim little lapdogs...

When I lived in the Borders, a fairly famous artist bought
a holiday home there, a former chapel. His wife was an
old schoolfriend of mine and we were both into long
country walks, and sometimes dragged Ian along with
us, though it really wasn't his thing. One day we were
crossing a field with my two Yorkies and we suddenly
realised Ian was just standing staring at one of them –
Boomer. We asked why and he said: 'Most people's Yorkies
have a red ribbon on their heads. Yours has a cowpat.'

I wonder if other dogs think poodles are members of a weird religious cult.

Rita Rudner

Designer Doggies

Designer dogs are the result of crossing two pure breeds. If you are contemplating a designer dog then you should research the characteristics of both its ancestral breeds, as such hybrids can inherit traits and behaviour from both of its pure-bred relations. If you find an aspect of one breed that wouldn't fit in with your lifestyle, then consider carefully before acquiring your oh-so-fashionable little friend. Increasingly popular, there are plenty of weird and wonderful woofers to choose from:

- Also known as 'Aussie-poo,' the Aussiedoodle is a poodle–Australian shepherd cross.

- A St Dane is a mix of Great Dane and St Bernard, resulting in a whopper of a dog.

- If the idea of owning a Muggin appeals then you'll be looking at a hound that is part miniature pinscher and part pug.

- A Wee-chon is a crossing of bichon frise and Westie.

Up in Heaven, St Peter, St Paul and Jesus decided that it would be fun to hold a dog show. 'Hmm, but we already have all the best breeds up here. There won't be any proper competition,' said St Peter.

'Relax,' said Jesus. 'I'm a man with a plan – we'll ask Lucifer to enter some dogs. He won't be able to resist trying to get one over on us.'

Lucifer was delighted with the invitation and accepted immediately. 'Of course, you realise that my dogs will wipe the floor with you boys,' he said with a devilish swagger.

'As if!' said St Peter. 'We have all the best breeds up here. How can your grotty mongrels beat us?'

'You're forgetting something,' said Lucifer, with a self-satisfied smirk. 'I have all the judges.'

Sit! Stay! Act!

*The best way to get a
puppy is to beg for a baby
brother – and they'll settle
for a puppy every time.*

Winston Pendleton

Ask Aunty Woofer

Dear Aunty Woofer,
We are thinking of buying a puppy for our daughter but know almost nothing about keeping a dog. Can you give me some puppy pointers?
Thank you.
From Lesley Holland

Dear Lesley,

A puppy is a big commitment and you should definitely do some research before you acquire one. Your best bet is to get a book out of the library, or go and visit your local dog rescue centre where they will be happy to give you advice. But here are just a few things that you need to know:

During its first week after birth 90 per cent of a puppy's time is devoted to snoozing, with the remaining 10 per cent spent on eating.

A puppy is born blind but begins to see when it is around two to three weeks old.

During the ages of between three and seven weeks a puppy's milk teeth will appear. Adult teeth start to come through between four and eight months of age. This is when you need to protect any precious furniture!

A puppy stops being a puppy and becomes an adult dog when it reaches one year of age.

And remember what Rudyard Kipling said: 'Buy a pup and your money will buy love unflinching.'

I hope this helps.

AW

Puppy Prep

If you want a sociable and stable dog then you should start training while your pooch is still in its puppyhood. After three months it is likely to be a much more difficult task, as by this time dogs are likely to display fear in new situations, resulting in a dog that is infinitely harder to train.

Speak to your vet for guidance on the best ways to socialise your dog, although do bear in mind that puppies can't be taken out until they have had all their vaccinations. However, it may be viable to expose them to experiences outside of the home – say, traffic noise – by taking them out in a pet carrier, thus enabling them to absorb smells, sounds and people. But do take professional advice so that your dog is not in any way vulnerable to infection.

Once they have had all their injections, the job of socialisation should continue. We all want our mutts to be good-tempered and reliable, as well as secure and unconcerned with the noise and hustle and bustle of everyday life. And while it is impractical to introduce dogs to every person or situation that they are likely to encounter in their lifetimes, the more experiences you can offer them in their early life the more confident they will be and less likely to develop phobias.

Try to include introductions between your dog and people of different height and size, colour, cultures, as well as those of disparate ages (from babies to grandparents), disabled people, people with facial hair, and those who wear uniform.

They should ideally be exposed to sounds spanning household noise (e.g. vacuum cleaner, domestic appliances, TV, etc.) and outdoors din (aeroplanes, traffic, people shouting and so on).

Prep School for Pups

With all new experiences, ensure that you make your dog feel secure and supported, and make sure that you are firmly in control. If pup senses that you are anxious then you will transmit your fear.

The most important thing is to begin training your new dog or puppy as soon as possible. The best way to train your dog is by attending specially designed courses that are run by experts, and reinforcing what you learn in class at home. But don't overdo it or your mutt will lose heart and interest. Keep sessions short and sweet, and always reward him once a new command has been learnt. Try to use hand signals with verbal commands, and keep commands clear and consistent. Above all, be patient. Some dogs take longer than others to catch on and teaching one command in each session is as much as you should aim for. Any more and you risk confusing your dog. Don't berate him if he gets it wrong or is seemingly a slow learner – and never, ever physically punish him, which could result in him becoming aggressive out of fear. Training sessions should take place somewhere there are minimal distractions – the park with other dogs and people milling about, and lots of interesting smells waiting to be sniffed, is not an environment that will be conducive to study. For details of classes in your area speak to your vet, or visit www.rspca.org/inyourarea or The Guild of Dog Trainers at www.godt.org.uk

Jump to it!

Dogs tend to jump up at people either in
'I'm-pleased-to-see-you' greeting, or because
they are simply overexcited. Either way, this
tendency needs to be nipped in the bud. The
most effective way to achieve this is simple:
ignore it. Completely. Don't meet their eye,
don't push them away and don't speak to
them. If they continue, walk away. Much like
the rule for boisterous children, the message
you should convey is that only good behaviour
will be rewarded, either with a treat or
with positive attention.

Training for the Spotlight

An animal trainer whose work includes training dogs for films, Martin Winfield of Rockwood Animals says there are three key factors in training a dog for the limelight: knowing that the dog has the right temperament (is sociable and at ease in the often hectic world of studios and movie sets); an awareness of the dog's limitations; and the acceptance that you will probably be bored rigid for much of the time.

'Filming especially can take a very long time. I once spent three days with a couple of Dobermanns filming an attack scene for a film with James Coburn. In those three days we shot just thirty-five seconds of film,' says Martin.

But if you think that your hound would respond well to training for the bright lights then Martin's advice is never to sign up with any agency that asks you to pay to do so.

'A good agent will represent your dog without charging a fee and they will have your dog's best interests at heart. I build a relationship with the dog and its owner, and on set I represent the voice of the dog. If a director tries to push an animal to do something that I don't think is right then I will say no on its behalf.'

DOG TALES

Nicky, a gardener and dogsitter, recalls a time when her love for Sushki the golden retriever was sorely tested. In a demonstration of misguided but nevertheless revolting behaviour, Nicky says: 'I accepted a big wet kiss from him – but unbeknown to me, until it was too late, he had the tail and back legs of a dead mouse sticking out of his mouth!'

Presumably Sushki was taking the Mickey...

The dog was created especially for children. He is the god of frolic.

Henry Ward Beecher

A Dog's Prayer...

Dear God,
When we get to Heaven, can we sit on your couch? Or is it the same old story?

Bullseye, Nana, Timmy and Dip: Literary Pups

*Let sleeping dogs lie –
who wants to rouse 'em?*

Charles Dickens, *David Copperfield*

Dogs have featured in some of the greatest literary endeavours of all time, but the very first author of canine literature is believed to be one Marcus Terentius Varro (116–27 BC).

A Roman scholar and philosopher Varro, who wrote prolifically on a broad range of subjects, including agriculture. Clearly a doggy person, in his work *De Re Rustica* he gives advice on different dogs, spanning everything from diet to training.

Meanwhile, in the King James Bible, dogs are mentioned on 14 occasions. The only dog mentioned by specific breed is the greyhound, which occurs in Proverbs 30:29–31:

> There be three things which go well, yea,
> Four are comely in going;
> A lion, which is strongest among beasts and
> Turneth not away for any;
> A greyhound;
> An he-goat also.

Paw Prints

In early tales and fables authors were inclined to give dogs human traits. In Aesop's *The Dog and the Shadow* fable, for instance, the moral is not to be greedy or to clutch at shadows.

And although *The Two Gentlemen of Verona* is Shakespeare's only play in which a dog features prominently (the cheeky mutt Crab, as described tenderly by the servant Launce), various breeds rate a name-check in some of his other plays: greyhounds in *Henry V*, spaniels in *Antony and Cleopatra*, mongrels in *Macbeth* and hounds in *A Midsummer Night's Dream*.

In the last two centuries literature featuring dogs as key characters has developed, with man's best friend often appearing as precisely that. Who can forget Bullseye, the dog belonging to nasty Bill Sikes in *Oliver Twist*, for example? According to Dickens the dog was vicious, having been ill-treated by Sikes, yet the book suggests that Bullseye remained fierce also in loyalty to his tyrannical owner.

And what about dear old Nana, the Newfoundland belonging to the Darling family in *Peter Pan* by J. M. Barrie? Said to have been inspired by Barrie's own dog, Nana threw back her head and howled to try and warn the Darling parents that the children were being spirited away by Peter. Having ignored Nana's efforts, Mr Darling was left so appalled at the loss of his children that he slept in the kennel in Nana's place until they were restored to him, safe and sound.

In *Memoirs from the House of the Dead*, Dostoevsky brilliantly evokes the ghastliness of life in prison and details his conversations with a prison dog, a confidante whose presence clearly gave him much needed comfort.

Jollier conversations were had between humans and dogs in Enid Blyton's books, the most famous doggy characters being Timmy from *The Famous Five* and Scamper from *The Secret Seven*. Both dogs were pets belonging to junior sleuths, who seemed to be as enthusiastic about cracking crime as they were of partaking of enormous meals. Often concluding with Scamper/Timmy barking in agreement with something said by the friendly policeman who had arrived to congratulate the clever kiddies, before settling down with a juicy bone – the canine reward for sniffing out the baddies – these dogs were undoubtedly the real heroes of their stories.

Ay, in the catalogue ye go for men;
  As hounds, and greyhounds, mongrels, spaniels, curs,
Shoughs, water-rugs, and demi-wolves, are clept
All by the name of dogs: the valued file
Distinguishes the swift, the slow, the subtle,
The housekeeper, the hunter, every one
According to the gift which bounteous nature
Hath in him closed.

 **William Shakespeare,** *Macbeth*

Romancing the Bone

The best-selling author of a series of racy 'bonkbusters', Jilly Cooper is a self-confessed dog lover and currently the owner of a rescue greyhound called Feather. Regularly including dogs in her novels, Jilly often gives her animal friends their own cast list at the front of the book, as well as using them to give some of her human characters redeeming qualities. The heavenly-looking but often quite objectionable hero Rupert Campbell-Black, who features in Jilly's 'Rutshire Chronicles', is forgiven for being a womanising bad boy by virtue of being a dog lover; his affection for his dogs making readers instantly forget what an utter cad he has been in the previous pages. Meanwhile, who can have remained dry-eyed when Gertrude, Taggie Campbell-Black's little mongrel, loses her life trying to protect a much-loved human?

Dogs are not generally apt to revenge injuries inflicted upon them by their masters; but Mr. Sikes's dog, having faults of temper in common with his owner, and labouring, perhaps, at this moment, under a powerful sense of injury, made no more ado but at once fixed his teeth in one of the half-boots. Having given in a hearty shake, he retired, growling, under a form; just escaping the pewter measure which Mr. Sikes levelled at his head.

Charles Dickens, *Oliver Twist*

Cute and Cuddly

Another tear-jerker, and one of the most famous doggy stories of all time, Sheila Burnford's *The Incredible Journey* was published in 1961 and made into a Disney movie in 1963. Telling the story of a Labrador, a bull terrier and a Siamese cat stranded hundreds of miles from home, their journey across the Canadian wilderness is one of courage and determination; a true celebration of the intelligence and loyalty that man's best friend is renowned for.

In modern-day children's literature dogs also feature heavily. Lynley Dodds' *Hairy Maclary from Donaldson's Dairy* has been a staple of nursery bookshelves since the first book was published in 1983, while *The Hundred and One Dalmatians* dates back to the 1950s. Perhaps now better known by children for the Disney film versions that Dodie Smith's classic book spawned, the original story remains a thrilling page-turner that continues to delight young readers.

When Spike Milligan wrote *Dip the Puppy* in 1974, it was intended simply as a story to amuse his young daughter. It has subsequently given many children enormous pleasure, each of them revelling in the story of a young pup who can't say 'bow wow' and who makes friends with a wizard called Mr Sloppy-Knickers and Nibbles the rabbit.

A Trumped-up Tale

Walter the Farting Dog is possibly the greatest aid to getting young boys reading that the world has ever known. Written by William Kotzwinkle and Glenn Murray and illustrated by Audrey Colman, these hilarious gas-fuelled tales of poor Walter always result in fantastic farty fun that children, but especially small boys, absolutely adore. Dedicated to all those who have ever been 'misunderstood', Walter has a knack of foiling baddies with his silent-but-deadly chuffs.

*The dog is a gentleman; I hope
to go to his heaven, not man's*

Mark Twain

Poetry of the Pooch

Man's best friend has provided inspiration for poets and lyricists for centuries. From schoolchildren to revered poets, pups and pentameter have given pleasure to millions. Perhaps one of the most famous doggy poems of all is Elizabeth Barrett Browning's 'To Flush, My Dog'. One of the most important poets of the Victorian age, Elizabeth is said to have adored Flush, who gave her great comfort as she battled with ill health.

Other dogs in thymy dew
Tracked the hares, and followed through
Sunny moor or meadow.
This dog only, crept and crept
Next a languid cheek that slept,
Sharing in the shadow.

Other dogs of loyal cheer
Bounded at the whistle clear,
Up the woodside hieing.
This dog only, watched in reach
Of a faintly uttered speech,
Or a louder sighing.

And if one or two quick tears
Dropped upon his glossy ears,
Or a sigh came double
Up he sprang in eager haste,
Fawning, fondling, breathing fast,
In a tender trouble.

And this dog was satisfied
If a pale thin hand would glide
Down his dewlaps sloping
Which he pushed his nose within,
After – platforming his chin
On the palm left open.

 Elizabeth Barrett Browning, from 'To Flush, My Dog'

Walkies!

The wonderful thing about having dogs is that it makes you go walking.

Pearl Lowe

Leading by Example

Walking with your dog is simply one of the greatest pleasures known to man, but make sure you use a lead where appropriate. This keeps your dog safe and reassures others that he is under control.

Ensure that your dog walks near your foot, but don't resort to pulling on the lead too much. The standard *heel* position is to your left, with your dog's head even with your leg, waiting for your signals.

For the lead that is best suited to your walking needs and your dog's proportions, speak to your vet or local pet shop, although generally speaking a retractable lead allows you to retain control while giving your dog a certain amount of freedom. When you let him off the lead, do so only in the sure and certain knowledge that he will come when called.

Picnickers are an extremely tempting sight for most dogs, but your dog needs to learn that picnic nicking is an absolute no-no. Nor should you allow him to eat anything that has been discarded on the path.

Bounty Hunting

Walking with your dog can sometimes turn into a veritable treasure hunt, even if it doesn't result in a tasty titbit. Dog walkers often show themselves to be good Samaritans, handing in wallets, keys and other valuables discovered by their four-legged friends.

One dog walker, Mrs Edmunds, recalls that her Labrador Oscar was especially adept at finding treasure. But as well as soft toys, shoes, umbrellas, a handbag, a pair of headphones and a baby changing mat, there was a day when Oscar added something to his collection that, technically, wasn't in fact lost.

'We were on one of our favourite walks; a lovely path surrounded by woodland. Oscar bobbed out of sight for a moment, only to reappear with something in his mouth. Clearly highly pleased with himself, he whisked about in a very jolly way, but I couldn't see what it was that he had found. But I then heard a yell and a chap in his birthday suit, followed by a giggling young lady whose clothes were decidedly askew, emerged from the undergrowth. Frantically covering his nudity with a stray carrier bag, the man yelled that Oscar had pinched his shorts, which contained his wallet and, more importantly, his pants! Of course, Oscar was thoroughly overexcited by the shouting and refused to let himself be caught, so the whole thing ended up being like one of those daft Benny Hill-type chases.

Eventually I cornered my naughty dog and made him drop his spoils. By then the three of us had a serious case of the giggles and we ended up finishing the walk together. Oscar is a very friendly dog and his two great loves are people and retrieving. He stumbled on a situation that combined both, and on that basis thought it was perfectly acceptable to interrupt the couple's afternoon tryst.'

DOG TALES

Spud Talbot-Ponsonby undertook an incredible
journey: walking the coastline of Britain in its
entirety with her dog Tess. In her book *Two Feet,
Four Paws*, Spud recounts her feelings as she
neared the end of the road...

Tess had waited on the muddy paths of Cornwall when I
had thought I could go no further. She had experienced
my Highland euphoria, and leapt the peat gullies with
sheer *joie de vivre*; she had pounded main roads, being
sprayed by polluted puddles; she had walked hundreds
of miles of empty beach; she had fallen in rock pools,
and communicated with foxes; she had learnt the laws
of nature, and had learnt to love the sea; she had played
in the snow, and sweated many miles; she had walked
through numerous eight-hour-long deluges; she had
chewed mayors' ears, and eaten their teas; she had made
photographers despair and wrestled with policemen;
she had made homeless people smile; she had loved the
drivers and made them each feel special; she had slept
in castles, Butlin's, grand hotels, haunted spare rooms,
mobile homes, guest houses and top floor flats.

She was a star.

Any woman who does not thoroughly enjoy tramping across the country on a clear frosty morning with a good gun and a pair of dogs does not know how to enjoy life.

Annie Oakley

F or several moments I just did not know what had
happened to me. It felt like a train crash. Forty-five
kilos of bone and muscle hurtling into me, the collision
made my top and bottom teeth clang together.

'You mad dog!' I managed to call out, even though I
was fighting to get my breath.

It was my first walk with Monty off the lead.

Barrie Hawkins, *Twenty Wagging Tales:*
Our Year of Rehoming Orphaned Dogs

A Walk on the Wild Side

Barking Sands beach can be found on
the Hawaiian island of Kauai. Known
for its unusually dry sand, it is said
that when you walk on it the sand
makes a sound like a barking dog.

Five of the Best Dog Walks

Hampshire: Village, River and Woods Walk

Taking between one and two hours depending on your pace, this circular walk takes you from Beaulieu village in the New Forest, along the river to Buckler's Hard and then through woods that bring you back to the village again. Affording stunning views of the river, woofers can cool down by taking a dip en route.

Kensington Gardens, London: Park and Pride

Of all the London parks Kensington Gardens is arguably the prettiest the capital has to offer. A beautiful circuit that has been the walk of kings and queens since 1536, it has also long been a favourite of city dwellers and their dogs.

Snape Marshes, Suffolk: Wellies and Wine Walk

Start from the main village crossroads, walking through the village until you reach a footpath on the right, which heads south and into the marshland. Taking in the nature reserves, the path enters woods, bringing you out on the north side of the River Alde. At Snape Bridge the path merges into the B1069, providing a pavement promenade back to the heart of the village. Conclude at the Crown pub for a well-deserved glass of wine.

Fife Coastal Path, including St Andrews West Sands Beach: Life's a Beach

Walking along this stunning bit of coast you can enjoy glorious sandy beaches, complete with rocks for dogs to sniff at and explore. Boasting cliffs, hills and flat areas, this is a stretch that you can enjoy either as a full afternoon's trek, or simply for a quick scoot and a breath of bracing sea air.

Whitcliffe Common, Ludlow, Shropshire: Housman's Home Turf

Located on the southern edge of Ludlow, Whitcliffe Common is owned by the Plymouth Estates. Originally part of a far bigger medieval common, it is a walk with enchanting views of Ludlow Castle, the river and the picturesque Shropshire countryside. Take binoculars and look across the county from the fantastic vantage point that the elevated route offers.

Ask Aunty Woofer

Dear Aunty Woofer,
I am undertaking a sponsored walk of some distance next summer and would very much like to take my golden retriever, Lottie, with me. I know she will adore the adventure, but I am worried about the heat and how best to cool her down. What do you advise?
L. Ayling, Durham

Dear L. Ayling,
What a splendid time you and Lottie will have! Retrievers are excellent company on long walks, especially if your route takes you via water, where she will no doubt give herself a cooling dip. Check with organisers to ensure that the walk does indeed take in any rivers, lakes or sea. Dogs can't sweat so in the summer it is vital to keep them cool and hydrated on walks. When you stop for breaks be sure to see that Lottie has a good drink herself; perhaps consider carrying a bowl with you that you can get filled at any pubs or shops you might be passing.
Kind regards,
AW

Remember...

- In the UK between 1 March and 31 July you MUST keep your dog on a short lead when walking over access land.

- Ensure that your dog is under proper control, especially in areas where there is livestock and wildlife.

- Leave only footprints and take nothing but photographs. (In other words, take your rubbish away with you and don't dig up plants to take home for your garden.)

Love Me,
Love My Dog

*If you are a host to your guest,
be a host to his dog also.*

Russian proverb

More Than Just a Wag and a Woof

In 2011 the findings of new research announced that the relationship between dogs and their owners is actually even closer than had been previously thought.

Researchers at Portugal's University of Porto have now concluded that dogs have greater human-like social skills than chimps. Dr Karine Silva claimed that in the course of the studies, researchers discovered that man's best friend gets as upset as young children when they witness familiar people in distress, even when the distress is faked.

Backing up the research are the reports of canines that, although untrained for such a purpose, intuitively come to the rescue of humans in emergency situations. This, says Dr Silva, suggests 'empathetic perspective-taking'.

But whatever the science behind the bond, to many people dogs are simply much more than pets; they are members of the family, in some cases even child replacements. George Clooney's partner Elisabetta Canalis stated in a press interview that she had no wish to become pregnant – 'My maternal desires are fully satisfied with my dogs,' she said.

As for the death of a much-loved dog, a 2011 survey for The Co-operative Pet Insurance found that one person in four agreed that the loss of a favourite pooch was every bit as traumatic as losing a close relative. In another poll, this time carried out by the American Animal Hospital Association, it was revealed that 33 per cent of dog owners admit to talking to their dogs on the phone, or leaving messages on an answerphone for them!

The greater love is a mother's; then comes a dog's; then a sweetheart's.

Polish proverb

DOG TALES

In *Toute Allure: Falling in Love in Rural France*, author Karen Wheeler describes how she lost her heart to Biff.

He's really adorable. I can't help thinking he would be the perfect size for my home: a little smaller than a cocker spaniel, but big enough to be a real dog rather than something that could be carried around in a handbag.

He's so cute. I've only known this little creature for a quarter of an hour and already I feel a massive spark of affection...

Until Death Them Do Part

In 1858 John Gray was buried in old Greyfriars Churchyard in Edinburgh. His dog, a Skye terrier, became known as Greyfriars Bobby and is said to have slept on his master's grave for the following 14 years until his own death. A statue now commemorates this little dog with the big heart that showed his master total loyalty.

> ### *Helen's Hounds of Love*
>
> Left blind and deaf following a severe illness
> as a baby, Helen Keller was a confirmed
> dog lover and owned several dogs during
> her lifetime. As a child she even tried to
> communicate with her beloved pooches
> by finger spelling into their paws.

A Force for Love

They say that love conquers all and for seven-week-old
German shepherd pup Jake a little love proved to be a
miracle cure. Found tethered to a lamp post where he
was being tortured by children with fireworks, officers
from the Northumbria Police took the terrified little
chap under their wing. Building up Jake's confidence
with lots of gentle loving care, by his first birthday Jake
qualified as a fully-fledged police dog.

Enough Love for All

Weighing in at 10 stone, Dave the Rottweiler probably wouldn't be your first choice of babysitter. But Dave is the archetypal gentle giant when it comes to those smaller than himself – and not even just those of his own kind. Photographed by a national newspaper in 2011 after he had been awarded the title of Most Inspirational Dog in a national competition, the snap showed Dave with three of his surrogate children; a rabbit, a quail and a kitten. His owner, who runs a pet shop, realised that Dave was a natural mother when she brought home an abandoned bunny. Before she could stop him, Dave had walked directly up to the little creature and had begun gently licking its face. They were soon sharing a water bowl and snuggling up together. Since then Dave has mothered all sorts of needy animals, including a fleet of ducklings. A rescue dog that had been horribly treated, Dave's early experiences seem to have left him intent upon proving that it is love that makes the world go round.

I love my dog and he loves me
We play beneath the cherry tree
We chase the wind, we run, we flee
He only stops to have a wee.

Louisa Rose, aged 7, about her rescue mutt, Sherlock

Pub Dogs

*If this dog do you bite, soon as
out of your bed, take a hair of
the tail the next day.*

Ebenezer Cobham Brewer

Dogs and pubs – especially country pubs – do seem to go together. In fact, walking into a typical country inn, with a traditional roaring log fire and a selection of fine ales, feels somehow wrong if there isn't a hound pottering around the bar. But while many pubs welcome our four-legged friends, not all do. Which is why Kate Crosby set up a website that lists pubs all over the country where dogs are assured as friendly a reception as their human companions. Initially something that she set up for fun, Kate was astonished when www.doggiepubs.org.uk started getting thousands of hits every week. Clearly there was a need for a comprehensive directory of dog-friendly pubs and this non-commercial resource is now seeing new pubs, in both the town and country, being listed daily by dog lovers who have enjoyed a hospitable hostelry in the company of their dog.

'Dogs are part of the family and a good dog-friendly pub should make your dog feel as welcome as you are,' says Kate. 'Dog bowls of water should be available, and perhaps even dog biscuits – some pubs even have a doggy menu.'

A Doggy Drop

An old English 'cocktail' dating back to the
early nineteenth century, a Dog's Nose
is not for the faint-hearted...

Ingredients:
12 oz ale
1 oz gin

Method:
Pour the gin into a beer glass, and then add the ale.
Serve accompanied by a slice of pork pie and a
smearing of English mustard.

Ding-dong Daisy of Bristol

'Time at the bar,' the familiar cry of landlords all over the country, is the indisputable signal that it is time to sup up and shove off. But lest the regulars of Ned Clarke's pubs be in any doubt, Daisy, his Jack Russell, makes sure that the message rings in their ears.

Taking her cue from her owner's vocal call of 'Time,' Daisy smartly leaps out of her basket onto a bar stool, and from there onto the bar itself. Gripping the rope on the bar bell tightly in her jaw, the little dog then rings the bell enthusiastically.

Having originally delighted locals at the Portcullis pub in Bristol, Daisy is continuing to play to a packed public house, as she and Ned have now moved to another pub in the city, The Three Tuns.

Explaining how Daisy, who he had bought as a puppy, took to her self-appointed role as bell-ringer, Ned said that it started with how she always seemed interested when the bell was rung. Evidently one day she simply sprang on to the bar and did the job herself, and quickly realised that it was a party trick that earned her a good deal of attention.

But with The Three Tuns located almost next door to Bristol Cathedral, one wonders if Daisy has her sights set on campanology on a bigger scale...

Bus to the Boozer

As an elderly gentledog of ten human years, Ratty the Jack Russell liked nothing better than popping into his local boozer for a few titbits and a bit of a scratch behind the ears from his chums.

What is unusual about Ratty and his visits to the pub is that his local was five miles away, a journey that the adventurous hound made alone... by bus!

Ratty's human Gary told the press how the lovable dog used to hop on the number 10 and travel to The Black Bull in York, where he was given pats a-plenty and as many sausages as his little belly could accommodate.

His fame spread far and wide, winning him fans as far away as Japan, and when a new landlord took over and barred Ratty from The Black Bull, the canny dog just changed his preferred local to a neighbouring pub, The Rose and Crown.

And for My Next Trick...

The King's Head pub in Chichester, West Sussex was once frequented by a canny Great Dane who not only blagged bar snacks from customers but also opened the packets himself.

Now a trendy bar and restaurant, the venue is still home to many locals who fondly recall how the dog would greet each punter, accompany them to the bar, and then look soulfully at them. Any newcomers unable to decipher the pleading look were quickly tipped off by the regulars that the huge hound was asking for a packet of crisps, ideally cheese and onion. On being presented with the packet the dog would lay on the floor, carefully positioning the packet between his front paws. Using one paw to anchor the bag, with his other he used his nails to 'pop' it, thus releasing the crisps.

As one drinker recalls: 'The crisps lasted approximately two seconds.'

Pedigree Pints

- British Bulldog is a full-bodied best bitter made with Whitbread Golding variety hops. This is a pint with a distinctive aroma and a flavour to savour.

- Bedlington Terrier from the Northumberland Brewery is a light-coloured ale with a definite bite to it.

- Sheep Dog Bitter, also from the Northumberland kennel, is a good, basic, tawny beer with a fruity tang.

- Other barking beers include Cornish Corgi, Dozy Dawg, Wet Nose, Nethergate Old Growler and Northumberland Sheepdog. Or perhaps if you are headed for the USA you could visit the Lucky Labrador Brewing Company?

Newcastle Brown 'Dog'

Nicknamed 'Dog' in its native Tyneside, Newcastle Brown acquired this seemingly unconnected handle from a euphemism used by locals who were sneaking out for a crafty bevy: 'I'm just nipping out to walk the dog' was shorthand for covert supping.

Prime-time
Pooches

I class myself with Rin Tin Tin.

Shirley Temple on her early screen success

Lucrative Lassie

Originally a short story by Eric Knight that was published in 1938, *Lassie Come Home* was then rewritten as a novel, instantly becoming a howling success and a best-seller.

An account of a loyal and courageous collie who bravely travelled hundreds of miles to 'come home' to her owner, it was a tale to tug at the hardest of heartstrings. In 1941 Hollywood's MGM studios bought the movie rights for $10,000. At the time this was deemed barking, as films with dogs in weren't considered to be big buck makers.

Casting a collie called Pal, the movie *Lassie Come Home* premiered in 1943 to critical acclaim. One of the most successful films at the box office that year, two young stars of the future were among the cast: Roddy McDowell and Elizabeth Taylor. To the delight of the movie's backers, the return was as brilliant as the reviews – and audiences were demanding more. Quick to capitalise on their success, MGM produced film after film – a series that spanned 50 years!

In 1947 the *Lassie* radio show took to the airwaves, followed soon after by the television show, which launched in 1954. Running for 17 years, this award-winning show took its place in the record books as one of the longest running television programmes in history.

A Collectable Collie

If you have any Lassie merchandise from
the films or TV shows languishing in the
loft then you could be sitting on a doggy
gold mine. Many pieces are now collector's
items and with Lassie fans all over the
world the market is highly competitive.

Pottering with Fang

Harry Potter dog, Fang, played by three different Neapolitan mastiffs, was brought to life by male dog Monkey in *Harry Potter and the Order of the Phoenix*. Belonging to Harry Potter's half-giant chum Hagrid, the big-screen Fang weighs in at a whopping 10 stone. Hugo, another of the mastiffs to have played Fang, once made a TV appearance with Fern Britton, during which he accidentally spat on her!

I have yet to see one completely unspoiled star, except for the animals – like Lassie.

Edith Head, movie director and designer

I was haunted by trainers going 'Up, up, up, get up'. You find yourself picking your head up and then realising, they aren't talking to me.

Jeff Daniels, about working on the film
101 Dalmatians

Toto's Sex Change

Perhaps one of the most famous dogs in film history, Terry the Cairn terrier played Toto in the 1939 film *The Wizard of Oz*, even though she was a bitch and not, as the film claims, a male dog.

An abandoned dog, Terry got lucky and was rescued by Carl Spitz, a dog trainer. Landing her first film role in the 1934 romance *Ready for Love*, Terry went on to star in several films, including *Bright Eyes with Shirley Temple*. In 1938 Terry was cast as Toto in MGM's production of L. Frank Baum's classic tale. To prepare for the role Terry lived with Judy Garland, who allegedly was so smitten with her canine co-star that she begged to adopt her. Carl Spitz refused, keeping her even when she retired from the limelight.

Terry went over the rainbow to doggy heaven in 1944 and was buried in the gardens at Spitz's kennels.

For her part as Toto in the original film of *The Wizard of Oz*, Terry the Cairn terrier was paid $125 a week. This was more than some of the film's human cast members.

A Canine Cockney

Wellard was one of the TV soap *EastEnders*' best-loved characters. Appearing between 1994 and 2008, this cockney hound was a Belgian Tervuran shepherd dog. Played by a dog called Kyte, in the show the character Robbie Jackson rescued Wellard from a master who ill-treated him. Leaving the show in a tear-jerking scene in which Bianca Jackson finds Albert Square's most famous canine looking suspiciously lifeless on the floor, Wellard is still sometimes referred to in *EastEnders* today.

The Blue Peter First

Petra was the first *Blue Peter* dog, introduced in 1962 when the producers decided to give the show a pet, so that young viewers who didn't have a dog of their own could at least have a share in the one that starred in their favourite telly programme. However, and most unfortunately for the BBC, the mongrel that was selected died after just one appearance. Mindful of distressing kiddies all over the country, a covert operation to find a lookalike began immediately and a suitable dog was discovered in a London pet shop. Petra remained on the show until 1977, when she retired due to ill health. News of her death later that year made national headlines. A statue of the programme's first canine can be found in the *Blue Peter* garden.

Nipping into Musical History

One of the most iconic images of the twentieth century, Nipper was the dog made famous by a record label. Pictured listening to a gramophone, Nipper – a smooth-haired fox terrier – became mascot, logo and trademark for the HMV brand. Painted by Francis Barraud, it wasn't until 1895, three years after Nipper's death, that Francis painted him in the world-famous pose. Entitling the painting *His Master's Voice*, the Royal Academy rejected it, which prompted him to patent the painting instead. He then offered the painting to the Gramophone Company, who bought it.

My name is Oprah Winfrey. I have a talk show. I'm single. I have eight dogs – five golden retrievers, two black Labs and a mongrel. I have four years of college.

Oprah Winfrey, when asked to describe herself during jury selection

Best in Show

dam:

[1] *a female dog with puppies.*

[2] *an expression, usually one of the politer ones, overheard at dog shows as losers leave the ring.*

The competitive nature of humans is undoubtedly responsible for kick-starting dog shows.

Having hitherto been mostly bred as workers, by the middle of the 1800s dogs were beginning to be appreciated for their appearance and personalities. In 1859, setters and pointers and their humans were invited to exhibit and compete at what is believed to be the first formal dog show in the world, held in Newcastle Upon Tyne.

The idea of a dog show quickly became highly popular, spreading right across the country. However, while any trend was usually swiftly picked up by our American friends, because of the Civil War America didn't see its first dog show until 1877 – now the oldest sporting competition bar the Kentucky Derby!

The Olympics of the canine world in Blighty is Crufts. Set up by Victorian gent Charles Cruft in 1891, it is now one of the biggest and most prestigious dog events in the world. Much more than just a competition, Crufts today is a tail-wagging festival that trumpets the special relationship between man and dog, and the multifarious roles that dogs play in our lives.

The first ever Crufts was staged at Islington's Royal Agricultural Hall where there were an impressive 2,437 entries. The Kennel Club took over as organisers of Crufts in 1948 and remains top dog of the event today. Crufts was first televised in 1950 and in 2000 Rescue Dog Agility was introduced to the programme, giving rescue dogs their opportunity to grab the limelight.

As well as 'proper' dog shows, which have classes for just about every kind of breed, along with classes for working dogs and competitions in agility, the fun dog show is also a staple of village fetes and the charity fundraising calendar. Here you can enter classes such as The Dog Most Like its Owner, The Dog with the Waggiest Tail and The Dog the Judge Would Most Like to Take Home.

Crufts' Top Dogs

- Named Crufts Champion in 2011, flat-coated retriever The Kentuckian, or Jet, as he is known outside of the show ring, beat no less than 22,000 competitors to win the prestigious title. Nine years old – that's 63 in doggy years – the elder statesdog is the oldest winner in Crufts history.

- The Best in Show prize has been awarded for the past 83 years, with 41 different breeds winning the sought-after title.

- Some previous top dogs at Crufts in more recent times include:

  Araki Fabulous Willy, a Tibetan terrier (2007)
  Caspians Intrepid, an Irish setter (1999)
  Starlite Express at Valsett, an English setter (1988)
  Burtonswood Bossy Boots, a St Bernard (1974)

Scooping the Prize for Best Bitch

While you would expect to find lots of bitches at dog shows, sometimes these are human in form, like the 'lady' who a stallholder at Crufts encountered at the NEC.

A woman with a Great Dane was strolling past when the dog decided to squat down and leave a very large deposit. The woman called out to the stallholder and asked her to 'keep an eye on this' while she went to get something to clean it up, in case anyone stepped in it. The kindly stallholder duly took up position beside the unsavoury pile and for the next half hour stood there, smiling sweetly at everyone who went by and telling them to be careful where they stood as she was 'just minding it for someone'. Eventually realisation dawned – the woman had no intention whatsoever of returning, surely making her the Best Bitch of the show.

On her way to an important dog show a breeder and her prize-winning Pekinese dogs suddenly ground to halt, just five miles from the showground. Having called the AA to come and get her back on the road the breeder had a sudden flash of inspiration. Flagging down a passing taxi, she bundled her four pooches into the back, handed the driver £100 in cash, and instructed him to take the dogs ahead to the show.

Still waiting for the AA an hour later, the breeder was bewildered to see the taxi heading back towards her. Flagging it down once again she addresses the driver: 'I gave you a hundred pounds to take them to the show – why are you back here?'

Grinning, the cabbie replies: 'But the tickets only came to fifty pounds, so I thought I'd take them ice skating now.'

I love my dog because...

even when I feel like the whole world is against me, her tail still wags in delight when I get home at the end of a difficult day.

My dog is medium height with big brown eyes
She doesn't bite, but she does chase flies
She loves to play, she loves to eat
She's brown and grey and has big fluffy feet

🐾 **Milly Luxford, aged 6, about her Border collie–Old English sheepdog cross, Suzie**

Royal Dogs

*Golf seems to be an arduous
way to go for a walk. I prefer
to take the dogs out.*

HRH Princess Anne

Regal Rovers Through History

- Pharaoh king Tutankhamun was just nine years old when he became King of Egypt in 1331 BC. Reigning for a decade, he died at the age of 19. The young king's mummy was discovered in perfect condition in 1922 and in his tomb a number of artefacts were found, including an ornate dog collar. The find suggests that King Tut's dog was precious to the boy king.

- She might have wanted the poor to eat cake, but Queen of France Marie Antoinette can't have been all that bad – she was a dog lover after all. Reputedly devoted to her pooch, a spaniel named Thisbe, what became of the dog after the queen had her head lopped off by the guillotine is unknown.

- Loyal and faithful to the end, Caesar, a terrier belonging to King Edward VII, walked behind His Majesty's coffin in the funeral procession.

Her Majesty's Pride and Joy

Her Majesty the Queen continues the long-standing royal affection for dogs. As far back as the seventeenth century, many portraits in the royal collection depict dogs and their regal owners, with some pets even captured on canvas alone. Royal canines span a wide variety of breeds, but it is the corgi that most people associate with our present queen.

Corgis were first introduced into the fold by King George VI in 1933, when he acquired a cutie named Dookie, which delighted the young princesses Elizabeth and Margaret. Dookie was joined soon after by a corgi named Jane, whose puppies Crackers and Carol also became part of the royal household. One of the Queen's favourite corgis was Susan, who was an eighteenth birthday present.

Currently the Queen owns four corgis – Monty, Linnet, Holly and Willow; and Candy, Cider and Vulcan, who are dorgis. Dorgis are part corgi and part dachsund.

Other modern-day imperial hounds include Tosca and Rosie, Jack Russells belonging to the Duchess of Cornwall.

*I dressed dear sweet little Dash
for the second time after dinner in
a scarlet jacket and blue trousers.*

Queen Victoria on her pet
Cavalier King Charles spaniel

*During the Prince's visit, King
Timahoe will be referred to only
as Timahoe, since it would be
inappropriate for the Prince
to be outranked by a dog.*

In correspondence between Richard M. Nixon
and White House staff on how to address the
president's Irish Setter, during a visit by Prince Charles

Noble by name by nature noble too
Faithful companion sympathetic true
His remains are interred here

🐾 **Inscription on the gravestone of Queen Victoria's
collie, Noble, who was buried in the grounds of
Balmoral Castle in 1887**

Henry VIII – the Sly Old Dog!

Old Mother Hubbard
Went to the cupboard
To get her poor doggie a bone,
When she got there
The cupboard was bare
So the poor little doggie had none.

The Old Mother Hubbard of the traditional rhyme is widely believed to be none other than Cardinal Wolsey. The chief statesman and churchman of Tudor history, Cardinal Thomas Wolsey incurred the wrath of King Henry VIII when he failed to secure the king's divorce from Catherine of Aragon. Serial groom Henry was keen to be rid of Catherine so that he could marry Anne Boleyn. In the famous rhyme Henry was the 'doggie'. The 'bone' was the divorce itself, while the cupboard was symbolic of the Catholic Church.

Here lies DASH, the Favourite Spaniel of Queen Victoria
By whose command this Memorial was erected.
He died on the 20th December, 1840 in his 9th year.
His attachment was without selfishness,
His playfulness without malice,
His fidelity without deceit.
READER, if you would live beloved and die regretted,
profit by the example of DASH.

**Epitaph on the gravestone of
Cavalier King Charles spaniel, Dash**

The Legend of Gelert

In the village of Beddgelert, North Wales, a touching tribute to a brave and faithful hound is engraved on the supposed grave of Gelert, the famed favourite hunting dog of Prince Llewelyn. It reads:

In the thirteenth century, Llewelyn, Prince of North Wales, had a palace at Beddgelert. One day he went hunting without Gelert, who was unaccountably absent. On Llewelyn's return, the truant, stained and smeared with blood, joyfully sprang to meet his master. The prince, alarmed, hastened to find his son, and saw the infant's cot empty, the bedclothes and floor covered with blood. The frantic father plunged the sword into the hound's side thinking it had killed his heir. The dog's dying yell was answered by a child's cry. Llewelyn searched and discovered his boy unharmed, but nearby lay the body of a mighty wolf which Gelert had slain. The prince, filled with remorse, is said never to have smiled again. He buried Gelert here. The spot is called Beddgelert.

I am his Highness' dog at Kew;
Pray tell me, sir, whose dog are you?

**Engraved on the regal collar of
the Prince of Wales's dog**

Working Woofers

When you and your beloved dog rely on each other for nearly everything, your love is multiplied to epic proportions.

Dianne Phelps

Used in therapy for people suffering with chronic illnesses, in clinical settings as comfort for the terminally ill, as guides and assistants for those with impaired sight and mobility, in defence, farming and even on rescue missions, dogs have a fantastic work ethic.

In domestic service 'turnspit dogs' were real culinary powerhouses, employed to turn a treadmill which was linked to a roasting spit or to a butter-churning can.

Shepherds and farmers have employed dogs for their natural herding ability for many years, too, even inspiring a television show, *One Man and His Dog*, which ran on the BBC for 23 years.

Historically used to locate people in the wake of an avalanche, St Bernards come under the heading of search dogs. Finding people in disaster situations, such as earthquakes and floods, these clever dogs do an invaluable job saving lives. During World War One dogs were used to locate the wounded, while in Italy today dogs are being taught to rescue swimmers who have got into difficulty.

Mush!

In 1925 Balto the Siberian husky led a team
of huskies on a very important mission.
Carrying diphtheria serum over 600 miles, the
hardy hounds ran from Anchorage to
epidemic-ridden Nome.

Three men in a pub are discussing how clever their dogs are. The first man claims his dog is so smart that he can add up.

'What is nine times eight, Barker?' he asks the dog.

Barker jumps up and quickly uses the leftover chips on his master's plate to make the numbers seven and two.

'Seventy-two! Well done, Barker,' says the man.

'Well, that is very clever, but I'm an architect and I have taught my dog to build,' says the second chap. Whistling to his dog Riley, the dog immediately launches into a frenzy of activity, reconstructing the Eiffel Tower entirely from beer mats.

The other two men are highly impressed. 'I too have taught my dog my trade,' boasts the third man, clapping his hands to wake his snoozing mutt. The dog yawns, and then briskly mounts the other two dogs. Having had his wicked way with Barker and Riley, he then eats the leftover chips.

The other two men are bewildered as to what trade the dog's actions might represent. Not so the barmaid: 'High sex drive and always freeloading? You're an actor,' she says.

> **I love my dog because...**
>
> having a dog is just like having a
> fluffy shadow.

*Gratitude: that quality which the
Canine Mongrel seldom lacks;
which the Human Mongrel
seldom possesses!*

Lion P. S. Rees

Every dog must have a soul
Somewhere deep inside
Where all his hurts and grievances
Are buried with his pride

🐾 **Anonymous, 'A Dog's Soul'**

Dogs in Space

In 1957 Laika, a stray mongrel, was chosen by scientists in the Soviet Union who wanted to confirm their belief that organisms from Earth could survive in space. To prove their point they sent the world's second artificial space satellite, *Sputnik 2*, into space with Laika on board. Attached to a life-support system, Laika (nicknamed Muttnik by the press) went into orbit. Evidently suffering no ill effects, even at an altitude of 2,000 miles, people all over the world mourned when her life-support system ran out of batteries just a couple of days into her incredible journey. A monument honouring fallen cosmonauts was erected 40 years on at Star City on the outskirts of Moscow. Here Laika can be seen alongside her fellow space travellers.

Rover to the Rescue

*Recollect that the Almighty, who
gave the dog to be companion
of our pleasures and our toils,
hath invested him with a nature
noble and incapable of deceit.*

Sir Walter Scott

It is, of course, fair and true to say that not all dogs are naturally friendly, but counterbalancing this are the stories that often pop up in the news about a dog making an amazing journey in order to be reunited with its human family, or of dogs who have bravely protected or even saved their humans – for instance, according to statistics from 2008, it is claimed five families from across the USA and Canada were rescued by their dogs when their houses were on fire.

DOG TALES

Chris, a recovering alcoholic,
credits a very special dog for his sobriety.

I was 29 years old and I had lost everything. I had no job, my wife had walked out, taking my little girls with her, and I didn't have a penny to my name. All that was left was a flat that I owed two months' rent on, a crate of strong beer, a bottle of scotch and my dog, Rufus.

I sat in the chair and drank myself stupid. I must have passed out, which is how I let my cigarette fall onto the arm of the chair. I vaguely remember being roused from my stupor by Rufus, who was jumping up at me and barking his head off. When I finally came to it was not a second too soon. I managed to stumble to the door and open it. The smoke was horrendous and the fireman who arrived soon afterwards – called by a concerned neighbour who, alerted by Rufus's frantic barking, had seen smoke leaking into the communal corridor – said that had I not been roused by my dog, we would have surely perished.

It was the mother of all wake-up calls and by the same time the next day I was sitting in my first AA meeting. I have not had a drink since; now 22 years.

Sadly Rufus went to that great woodland walk in the sky some years ago, but I will never forget him. Whenever I tell this story to newly recovering alcoholics I fondly refer to him as my guide dog for the blind drunk. Without him I would be dead and instead I am sober; a good parent and grandparent and a useful member of society.

To your dog, you are the greatest, the smartest, the nicest human being who was ever born. You are his friend and protector.

Louis Sabin

Brave, Bold and Barking

- Leo, a poodle from Texas, saved his young master Sean's life. Throwing himself between a five-and-a-half-foot diamondback rattlesnake and Sean, allowing the child to escape, Leo was badly bitten by the venomous reptile. Teetering on the brink of life and death for a while, his fighting spirit saw this gutsy little dog make a complete recovery.

- Barry, a St Bernard, is believed to be the breed's most successful rescuer, having saved more than 40 lives.

- English bulldogs are not noted for their swimming skills, nor do they like cats any better than other breeds, but Napoleon bucked both trends when he plunged into a lake and swam out to retrieve a sack containing six abandoned kittens. Thanks to the bravery of their hero hound, four of the kitties survived.

- Heroic and highflying, a wire fox terrier called Igloo accompanied Admiral Richard Byrd when he made his flights over both the North and South Poles.

DOG TALES

Guide dog Yaron's human Jon Hastie of West
Kirby, Merseyside was amazed when his
incredible hound went above and beyond his
guide dog duties to rescue a little girl
from danger...

On holiday with family, Jon's black Labrador–golden
retriever cross, Yaron, accompanied the family in order
to fulfil his usual role of guiding his blind owner.

On the beach one day, Charlotte, Jon's seven-year-old
niece, toppled off her bodyboard into the sea. Swiftly
the current caused her to drift, and with no life jacket
she began to panic. Seeing the little girl in danger,
Yaron threw himself into the sea and began swimming
towards her. On reaching Charlotte the clever dog swam
in circles around her, enabling her to catch hold of his
collar. Calmly, Yaron then towed Charlotte safely back
to shore.

Yaron's heroics saw him named as the Beyond the Call
of Duty Guide Dog of the Year 2008 at the Guide Dog of
the Year Awards.

But sometimes it's the dog that needs rescuing. Frankie's human, Amanda, recounts a gentle stroll that became a grave situation of canine chaos.

I have a gentle giant who is the perfect family pet apart from his gigantic size – he is a wolfhound–bearded collie cross.

Waiting for my car to be serviced, I decided to have a picnic for me and Amy, my baby. We came across a lovely old churchyard where there were some benches. Rather than letting Frankie off his lead I kept him tied to the bench, as I thought it wasn't quite the thing to do to let him roam between the gravestones. Then the vicar came along, stopped to talk to me and asked why the dog was tied up. I explained, but the vicar said he liked to think the churchyard was for the living as well as those who had passed away and he didn't mind dogs in there at all, providing they were well-behaved and owners cleared up any mess they left. So I let Frankie free and he bounded away.

Almost immediately I heard the most horrendous crash and then pathetic howling. Leaving Amy in the charge of a concerned lady who was passing by, I followed the sound of the howling. A grave had been dug for a funeral later that day and had been covered with a large sheet of corrugated iron. Frankie had bounded onto that, it had given way and my poor dog was now at the bottom of the grave. Quite a crowd gathered, making various suggestions, but eventually someone remembered that a builder was working on a nearby house, so he was summoned with ladder and he and a workmate at last managed to lift Frankie out. The vicar's wife had come out to see what all the commotion was about and, seeing my dishevelled and flustered state, rushed back to the vicarage to return with a cup of hot, sweet tea for me. I was so grateful but as I put it down on the bench beside me, Frankie promptly buried his nose in the cup and slurped up every drop.

Ask Aunty Woofer

Dear Aunty Woofer,
My granddaughter is doing a school project on dogs, and
I was telling her what little I knew about Battersea Dogs
Home. I wondered if you knew anything about this most
excellent canine rescue centre – when it was founded, for
instance?
   Thank you very much.
   Molly Wickham

Dear Molly,
Battersea Dogs & Cats Home was established in 1860
by a smashing lady, Mrs Mary Tealby. Mrs T was very
worried about the huge number of animals roaming the
streets of London, so she set up what was then known
as 'The Temporary Home for Lost and Starving Dogs'.
Located in Holloway, North London, the organisation
moved to Battersea in 1871 and has been there ever since.
   To give you an idea of how many dogs are looked after
by Battersea, in 2009 they cared for 10,105 dogs.
   I hope the project is a howling success!
   AW

Dogs of War

What counts is not necessarily the size of the dog in the fight – it's the size of the fight in the dog.

Dwight D. Eisenhower

Dogs have, throughout history, been used in warfare. During the days of the Roman Empire formations of dogs were kitted out with armour or vicious spiked collars and then were sent onto the battlefield to attack the enemy.

- In his campaigns Attila the Hun used giant Molossian dogs, predecessors of the mastiff, while in the Middle Ages dogs were often used to defend caravans.

- During the Seven Years War, Russian dogs were utilised as effective messengers and, horrendously, as suicide bombers. Napoleon used dogs as sentries at the gates of Alexandria, relying on the dogs to alert his troops in the event of an attack.

- The first recorded American Canine Corps was during the Seminole War of 1835, and again in 1842 in Florida and Louisiana, where the army used bloodhounds to track American Indians and runaway slaves.

- Harnessing the frontline abilities of the dog, in 1884 the German Army established the first military school for training war dogs.

This soldier, I realised, must have had friends at home and in his regiment; yet he lay there deserted by all except his dog. I looked on, unmoved, at battles which decided the future of nations. Tearless, I had given orders which brought death to thousands. Yet here I was stirred, profoundly stirred, stirred to tears. And by what? By the grief of one dog.

Napoleon Bonaparte, who on discovering a dog beside the body of his dead master, licking his face and howling on a moonlit battlefield, remained ever haunted by this scene

The Dickin Medal

A bronze medallion inscribed with the words 'For Gallantry' and 'We Also Serve', the Dickin Medal hangs on a ribbon. Striped green, dark brown and pale blue the ribbon represents water, earth and air – the naval, land and air forces.

Established during the Second World War by founder of the PDSA (People's Dispensary for Sick Animals) Maria Dickin CBE, the unique medal was introduced to honour animals' devotion to man and duty, and is awarded to animals displaying bravery in the line of duty while serving or associated with any branch of the armed forces or civil defence units.

For Queen and Country

In World War Two dogs were trained to perform sophisticated tasks for special missions, working as messengers, sentry dogs and even mine detectors. Judy, an English pointer, was recruited to serve on a Royal Navy vessel due to her ability to hear hostile aircraft long before any of the human crew could. Unfortunately, the vessel she was assigned to sank during a battle and the crew were captured. Judy somehow gained access to the POW camp where they were held and helped the men by fetching them scraps of food. Despite the best efforts of the Japanese prison guards to shoot her, Judy managed to escape and, thanks to the efforts of one RAF serviceman, Frank Williams, she was registered as an official prisoner of war – the only animal in history to receive this status.

Treo the Brave

In 2010 Treo, an Army sniffer dog, received the highest accolade given to animals: the Dickin Medal.

The brave black Labrador has saved the lives of hundreds of troops and civilians thanks to his brilliant nose, which can sniff out a Taliban bomb with ease.

Working in the unforgiving heat of Afghanistan, very often with enemy fire ringing out all around him, the eight-year-old hound hero was part of the Working Dog Support Unit, Royal Army Veterinary Corps.

Presented with his medal, the animal equivalent of the Victoria Cross, by Princess Alexandra, Treo was the sixty-third animal to receive the honour and joins the 26 other dogs who have been recipients of the prestigious decoration.

Now retired and enjoying life as a family pet, Treo uses his expert nose for sniffing out treats rather than deadly explosives.

He is the one 'person' to whom I can talk without the conversation coming back to war.

Dwight D. Eisenhower on his Scottie dog

Cry, 'Havoc!' and let slip the dogs of war.

William Shakespeare, *Julius Caesar*

Broken-hearted Hero Hound

When explosive search dog handler Lance Corporal Liam Tasker was paired with Theo, a springer spaniel cross, it was a match made in heaven. The two formed an immediate bond and were described as being made for each other.

In five months in Afghanistan the pair saved countless lives, finding more bombs than any of their colleagues. But in February 2011 the dream team was cruelly torn apart when 26-year-old Liam was killed by the Taliban, shot dead during a firefight.

Just days afterwards Theo, who was not quite two years old and was in the fullness of health, suffered a seizure and died. Without his beloved master, Theo's spirit and heart were broken. 'They always led the way so that others may be safe,' said Liam and Theo's Commanding Officer.

Warned by Woofing

> Hark, hark, the dogs do bark
> The beggars are coming to town
> Some in rags and some in tags
> And one in a velvet gown.

A rhyme that is traced back to thirteenth-century England, the origins of 'Hark, Hark, the Dogs Do Bark' echoes the wariness with which communities received strangers.

At that time beggars and wandering minstrels travelled from place to place. Coded messages of rebellion were relayed to the common people in the words of the medieval poets' ballads and rhymes, thus passing on the propaganda of the day from community to community.

These secret messages led to dastardly plots and uprisings against royalty, the church and politicians. Because of this cunning-but-musical means of gossip and rabble-rousing strangers were treated with suspicion, and it was the barking of their dogs that warned villagers and townsfolk of visitors, hence the opening line of this old rhyme.

Din-Dins

The dog's kennel is not the place to keep a sausage.

Danish proverb

The proverbial dog's dinner has come a long way since the first commercial dog food went on sale over a hundred years ago. Now comprising a dizzying array of products and ranges, the choice is vast. But the simple rule of thumb is that just like human beings, dogs need a balanced diet, with plenty of clean, fresh water available at all times.

Puppies generally require more calories to support them through their significant growth stage, while an older dog, which is perhaps not getting as much exercise, will need fewer. If you are in any way unsure about the do's and don'ts of feeding your dog then consult your vet, who will advise you so that you can ensure that your canine pal is receiving the right mix of nutrients and the appropriate quantities of food.

Please remember that human food is not recommended, and that chocolate in particular is very bad for dogs – potentially fatal if given in large quantities.

Did you hear about the dog that ate nothing but garlic?
His bark was much worse than his bite!

*To live long, eat like a cat,
drink like a dog.*

German proverb

Porky Pooches

Shockingly, a recent survey carried out by animal charity the PDSA revealed that in the UK 2.4 million dogs are fed scraps and leftovers as their main food source, with 7 per cent of dogs fed human chocolate. Many dogs suffer from being obese and current statistics suggest that as many as one in three dogs are overweight, putting them at risk of serious illness.

It is always advisable to reconsider your dog's nutritional requirements as he progresses from puppy to dog, and then at regular intervals as he ages. By tailoring his diet so that he continues to eat well and wisely, you will be keeping Fido as fit as a butcher's dog!

Ducking Down

A Staffordshire terrier pup called Ozzie from Cubbington was trying to stop another dog nicking his toy – a small plastic duck. Eventually, sure that the other dog was going to nab it, Ozzie took matters into his own... jaws. Scoffing the toy for safe keeping, the poor pooch needed surgery to remove his quackers chum, which one imagines might have been somewhat eye-watering to pass.

I gazed at the plate, empty on one side. I was sure there had been a sausage left. And where was Monty? I leaned over the arm of the chair to look round the room. There, under the table, half-hidden by a tablecloth, I could see an enormous black dog, silently licking his lips.

 Barrie Hawkins, *Twenty Wagging Tales: Our Year of Rehoming Orphaned Dogs*

Fine Doggy Dining

In March 2011 Laura Hothersall from Wiltshire revealed in a national newspaper feature that she spent approximately £50 a week on luxury food for her boxer, Harvey. Organic dog biscuits, organic sirloin steak, and a full roast dinner on Sundays, the pampered pooch evidently tucks into his upmarket diet with gusto, even wolfing down sprouts and roast spuds.

Number Crunching

In the USA Nero, a Dobermann–Great Dane cross, was rushed to the vet having wolfed down his owner's mobile phone. An operation to remove the phone got Nero 'off the hook' and he made a full recovery. Which is more than can be said for the phone.

Stone Me!

Vivian Cooper was very surprised when, on throwing a ball for her dog Mia, a two-year-old German shepherd–greyhound cross, she heard a fearful rumble coming from Mia's tummy. Likening the sound to marbles rattling in a pocket, Vivian rushed her pet to an animal sanctuary to be X-rayed. The result might well have caused her to exclaim 'Stone me!' as Mia was carrying ten rocks in her gut. Pinched from the fountain in Vivian's back garden, the daft hound had clearly developed a taste for the decorative stones, which by all accounts were as big as chicken eggs. Fortunately they were smooth, and so did not damage Mia's stomach lining.

Hound
Horoscopes

*The more I see of men,
the more I admire dogs.*

Jeanne-Marie Roland

Buddha Buddies

Even if you're a dedicated cat lover, nobody can dispute the fact that dogs are the most loyal and devoted of animals. In the Buddhist faith it is believed that on the day of Buddha's death, he summoned all animals to him. Legend says that only a dozen species came to his side before he died, dogs included. Evidently Buddha rewarded those who answered his call by giving them each a year of their own; hence the cat does not feature in the Chinese zodiac!

Aries dog says... I'm in charge!

Make no mistake. If you have an Aries dog then you will have to assert yourself as pack leader. Dither, and this canny canine will usurp you and proclaim himself top dog before you can say 'walkies'. Talking of which, this sign of the doggy zodiac needs plenty of exercise, as he has endless energy. Best human signs for Aries dog: natural leaders Leo and Sagittarius are the most compatible owners for this pushy pooch.

Taurus dog says... home is where the heart is (and with a bit of luck, the liver, dog chews and a nice big bone too).

Taurus dog likes his home comforts. Prone to laziness and greed (Taurus dog has a tendency to tubbiness) he is, however, a good-tempered woofer. An ideal family pet, he is also a music lover, so if leaving him home alone make sure you leave him with the radio on, preferably tuned to Classic FM (Taurus dog has highbrow tastes and does not appreciate Lady Gaga). Best human signs for Taurus dog: his laid-back nature makes him compatible with most human signs of the zodiac.

Sacred Dogs

The tombs of ancient American Indians have been found to contain hundreds of dog remains. Buried alongside people, with jewellery and chattels, it appears that dogs were regarded as escorts into the next world.

Pharaoh's Favourite

Originating in the Middle East, the saluki was a favourite of the pharaohs of ancient Egypt. These dogs were often found mummified along with their masters in tombs that date back to 2000 BC.

Gemini dog says... I'm exhausting, but you love me!

Easily bored but utterly charming, Gemini dog is nosy, smart and has bags of energy. But the downside of owning a Gemini dog is that if you don't give him an outlet for that boundless energy and creativity he will become twitchy and potentially destructive. Powerful Leo is probably the most suitable master or mistress for a Gemini woofer, being someone that the dog can accept as pack leader.

Cancer dog says... but my shrink invites me to get up on the couch.

Arguably the most patient of the barking zodiac, he is sensitive and prone to mood swings – playful and frolicsome one minute, hangdog and sulking in his basket the next. There are two great loves of his life: home and water. Loyal and affectionate, Cancer dogs are often very able when it comes to some sort of specialist training. Pisces humans usually make the most appropriate owners, being receptive and relaxed around neurosis.

Leo dog says... look at me! I'm Top Dog!

The emperor of the canine zodiac, give Leo an inch and he'll take at least 50 miles and then expect you to applaud him for doing so. But Leo is very charismatic, as well as brave. He tends to be a good-looker, whatever his breed, and so is a good choice for an owner wanting to get involved in the show scene. Fiercely loyal, this woofer will go to any lengths to protect his family. Aries and Sagittarius humans tend to bond best with the Leo dog.

Virgo dog says... let me do it, please!

The most happily domesticated of the canine signs, Virgo dog loves being your pooch. Not blessed with a great deal of imagination, being told what to do suits him, as it saves effort on his part. Virgo dog is probably the best sign for an owner who already has cats, as Virgo hound is very laid-back about feline companions. Compatible with almost all human star signs, Scorpio is perhaps the least well matched, as they usually regard poor Virgo dog's efforts to please as toadying.

The Dog-loving Prophet

Zoroaster, a Persian prophet, believed that the life of dogs was as important as that of human beings. He decreed it a sin to deny a dog food while humans ate.

The Year of the Dog

In the Chinese zodiac those born in the year of the dog are regarded as the givers in life, prepared to sacrifice their own dreams, ambitions and desires for the sake of others.

Libra dog says... more food, fewer walks and a comfy bed, please.

A gentle soul that expects affection and loyalty to cut both ways, Libra dog is keen to please. But be warned: he is on a one-dog mission to have the finer, more human things in life. Generally lazy, there is one area in which this woofer doesn't mind expending energy. The most sexually active of the canine zodiac, if you have a Gemini bitch and weren't planning on puppies then a trip to the vet sooner rather than later is advised. A Leo owner would probably be the best match for Libra dog.

Scorpio dog says... I'm practically perfect in every way.

With an extremely high opinion of himself, Scorpio dog has the waggiest tail of them all. He is also a complex personality. Love him and you will get that love back in spades, but if you do anything that he doesn't like, even for his own good, then woe betide you! Scorpio dog is also an excellent night watchman; on red alert at the smallest noise. But alert doesn't translate into fierce, so be prepared to face Burglar Bill alone, while your pooch hides under the duvet. A human Scorpio is the ideal partner for a Scorpio canine, as there is empathy and common ground.

Sagittarius dog says... woof woof, neigh!

Another tricky canine sign to comprehend, Sagittarius dog is restless, resourceful, and something of a conundrum. Seemingly part-dog and part-horse, he adores walks that require real physical exertion, like obstacles to jump over in the manner of a Grand National contender. Plucky and big-hearted, Sagittarius dog makes an excellent assistance dog. He is also very adept at learning tricks, which he will love to show off. Independent and with a passion for excitement, this hound is best partnered with an Aries owner, another sign with an adventurer's spirit.

Capricorn dog says... I've got your number.

Capricorn dog will form a swift opinion of you and will see through any attempts to dupe him. An agreeable pet, he is happy to work hard, but not always quick to do so. A bit of a social climber, with age comes an expectation of greater comforts and increased affection. But Capricorn dog does understand the need for a pack leader and will settle very quickly with human owners. The best match would be someone in a royal household, which would facilitate this dog's nose for the high life, but otherwise a Capricorn owner will be the most rewarding partnering.

Aristotle Goes to the Dogs

In ancient times dogs were championed by the likes of the philosopher Aristotle. 'There is honour in being a dog,' said the great man.

Aquarius dog says... nice to see you, to see you, nice!

Of all the performing dogs in the world, Aquarius dog is the one that most enjoys the limelight. As a TV star, in photographic shoots or even as part of a circus, he is a natural showman and a bit of an applause junkie. But he is also a team player and loves to run with the pack. For this reason the Aquarius dog owner should allow him off the lead whenever practical. Quick to make friends, walks will see you being followed by an entourage, as all Aquarius dog's chums come and say hello. Gemini and Libra will work well as human owners for Aquarius dog.

Pisces dog says... it's complicated.

Poor Pisces dog isn't the smartest ball in the basket. But he feels things deeply, which leaves him unsure and often insecure. On the plus side, he is a real people-pleaser, making him a lovable fellow. Playful and energetic, he is a terrific walking companion, although a great water lover. Expect your pooch to seek out ponds, puddles and paddling pools. Indeed, Pisces dogs have been known to try and join their owners in the bath or shower! Cancer and Scorpio are the best owners for Pisces dog.

A woman went to the cinema to see a romcom. In front of her she was surprised to see a man and his dog, seated side by side. The film began and the woman was amazed to see the dog responding to it: in the tear-jerking scenes it wept, and in the comic parts it laughed raucously. At the end of the film the woman was so enchanted by the movie-loving mutt that she went to speak to his owner.

'That is just the most incredible thing I have ever seen,' she said, patting the dog. 'He really did seem to enjoy the film.'

The man turned to her, nodding in agreement, and said, 'Yup, it really is amazing. He absolutely loathed the book.'

Give a Dog
a Bad Name

*Oh, what is the matter with
poor Puggy-Wug?*

Winston Churchill

Naming your dogs, like naming your children, should never be a rushed decision. Of course, it is important to choose a name that you like, but do take into consideration factors like your dog's personality type, as calling a boisterous, bouncing Labrador 'Serenity' would be ludicrous. Ben, a vet, and human to mongrels Guinness and Scrumpy, has some sound advice when it comes to the name game:

I always advise clients that before they give their dog a name they should open their back door and shout their preferred choice a few times to see how it sounds. It's amazing how many people change their minds once they have yelled 'Sexy Rexy' or 'Buggerlugs' within earshot of other people. Plus, if you pick a long name then you'll find hollering something like 'Knickerbockerglorious' a time-consuming pain when you are trying to get your dog to be obedient. The shorter the name, the quicker your dog will learn it, so I would recommend sticking to names of one or two syllables.

It is also advisable to avoid names that sound like a command. Believe it or not there are people who have christened their poor dogs names like 'Sit' and 'Drop'. Another idea is to check what names currently feature in the top ten lists and, if you can, steer clear of them. It will make your life a whole lot easier when you need to call your dog in a busy park if you aren't shouting the same name as half a dozen other dog owners.

Choosing a name that will still suit after your puppy becomes a grown-up dog is another consideration. Ickle Tiddles, Babykins and Pupperlicious will make you and your dog look utterly daft once they have left their puppyhood behind and you are still shouting a singularly inappropriate baby name at a 9-stone Great Dane.

Famous Fido

An old Latin name meaning 'I am faithful', the name 'Fido' became widely popular during President Abraham Lincoln's term of office, as this was the name of the President's own dog. Today 'Fido' is a general name used to describe any dog.

What's in a Name?

If you are registering a dog with the Kennel Club (which gives you access to a wealth of doggy information and enables you to take part in a wide range of shows and events) then certain rules apply. For instance, the name must consist of more than one word but not exceed 24 letters. Furthermore, a name which conflicts with an approved current Kennel Club name granted to another dog owner will not be accepted, nor can a registered name be repeated within a breed.

In recent times the trend for giving dogs human names rather than the traditional doggie names like Fido and Rover has escalated; no doubt a reflection of how much a part of the family we regard our dogs. In 2010 the top dog names in the UK, according to AA Pet Insurance, were as follows:

1.	Molly	6.	Holly
2.	Charlie	7.	Millie
3.	Poppy	8.	Daisy
4.	Alfie	9.	Jack
5.	Max	10.	Oscar

Some more ridiculous names include:

Pickle Von Corndog	Dog Vader
Lord Chubby Pruneface	Flopsy Squeakerton
Big Girl's Blouse	Basket
Pussy Galore	Shagger
Molly McBoozehound	Barnaby Bones

If you want a name that reflects your dog's personality then look at baby naming books or websites, as these often include a description of where the name comes from and what its meaning is. For example, Sam means 'listener', while Max translates from the Latin for 'the greatest'.

Talking to her class of eight-year-olds, the teacher said: 'Some plants have the word "dog" as the prefix. For instance, did you know that there is the dogrose, the dogwood, the dog violet? Now, who can give me another plant prefixed by "dog"?'

At the back of the classroom Jimmy leaps up. 'Me, Miss! I can,' he yells.

'Collieflower!'

Ask Aunty Woofer

Dear Aunty Woofer,
Please can you tell me where the phrase 'raining cats and dogs' stems from? I thought about it on a recent walk with my spaniel, Mr Magic, and it's been bothering me ever since.

Yours truly,
Mr Mark Davidson

Dear Mr Davidson,
This curious phrase dates back to seventeenth-century England when many dogs and cats drowned during heavy rain and when rivers burst their banks. The bodies of cats and dogs were often spotted as they were carried by flood tides that swept through towns, thus giving the impression that it had, quite literally, rained down cats and dogs.

I hope this sets your mind at ease and leaves you free to enjoy your walks with Mr Magic wholeheartedly now.
AW

Doctor Dog

There is no psychiatrist in the world like a puppy licking your face.

Ben Williams

Jab's the Job

As a responsible dog owner, you will know that making sure your special friend is up to date with all his vaccinations and booster injections is crucial. If you are in any doubt as to whether your dog has had all the shots he needs, consult your vet.

Genetically Programmed

Certain breeds are prone to genetic diseases and you would be well advised to do your homework on these before choosing your dog. Pure-bred, or pedigree, dogs are most likely to inherit a genetic disorder or disease.

Skin and Bones

Skin problems occur for a number of reasons. Allergies can be the result of foods that don't suit a dog, so keep an eye on his diet and any unusual reactions to food. Unwanted visitors such as fleas, ticks and mites are common triggers for canine skin problems. Regular grooming and bathing is the most effective way of keeping such irritations at bay.

Orthopaedic problems such as hip dysplasia can be genetic. As a dog gets older he, just like you, becomes more vulnerable to degenerative diseases like arthritis. Treatment for dogs is much the same as it is for humans suffering with such afflictions and your vet will prescribe anti-inflammatory drugs.

10 Physical Facts About Your Best Friend

1. Ear infections are one of the most common ailments in dogs. Most dogs have ears that flop, thus creating a warm and moist environment in the inner part of their ear; the perfect condition for bacteria and fungus to flourish.

2. Dogs have a visual range of 250 degrees. Humans have a visual range of 180 degrees.

3. A dog can hear sounds 250 yards away. Most humans cannot hear beyond 25 yards.

4. Dogs have twice as many muscles than people have for moving their ears.

5. Dogs take between 10 and 30 breaths every minute.

6. A dog's heart beats between 70 and 120 times a minute (a human heart beats 70 to 80 times a minute).

7. A dog's temperature is between 100.2 and 102.8 °F.

8. Fungal diseases like ringworm and hookworm are common in dogs but are easily treatable. A regular worming programme is the most effective way to reduce the chances of infection.

9. High-fibre, low-fat diets are believed to be beneficial to dogs suffering with pancreatitis.

10. In dim light a dog's sight is better than a human's.

Open Wide

Brushing your dog's teeth is an important part of keeping him healthy and should be done regularly to remove plaque and prevent bad breath. A human toothbrush is the best tool for the job; an adult toothbrush for large and medium breeds, a child's for smaller breeds. Use a specially designed pet toothpaste, and give him a safe chew toy, which will help keep teeth strong and clean. You should regularly check his mouth for signs of any problems and your vet should check his teeth once or twice a year.

Life in the Old Dog Yet

It is claimed that people who keep dogs tend to live longer than those who do not. It is believed that the calming influence of the company of man's best friend results in lower blood pressure, which in turn reduces the risk of heart attack.

Ask Aunty Woofer

Dear Aunty Woofer,
Why is it that when I'm staggering downstairs at stupid o'clock in the morning, shivering when the cold rain sweeps in on me as I step outside in my jim jams, my devoted pal then runs back up to his cosy bed, effectively saying, 'It's OK Mum, I've changed my mind now, it's too cold'?
   Yours sincerely,
   Mrs Brickie, Chichester

Dear Mrs Brickie,
There is a very simple answer to this query: because he can!
   AW

Loo Roll and
Labradors

*Whoever said you can't buy
happiness forgot little puppies.*

Gene Hill

Many advertisers have used dogs in their commercials. As well as pet stores and pet food manufacturers, there are numerous companies who have played the canine card to grab the consumer's attention. Banks, cars, insurance companies – dogs are a great sales tool. Big dogs like St Bernards are cast to imply strength, while traditional family dogs like Labradors are used to promote products and services that are aimed at children and families.

Since the first puppy advert had us all going gooey in 1972, there have subsequently been an incredible 130 adverts starring the loo-roll-thieving Labrador cutie, Andrex.

Every Home Should Have One

Created by ad agency The Red Brick Road for the marketing body Thinkbox, the advert that won almost as many fans as the golden puppies starred Harvey, the mutt who promoted the benefits of TV advertising by... making an advert! The premise went something like this:

> A couple are at a rescue centre to choose a dog. They see a couple of cute-looking dogs, when suddenly Harvey grabs their attention by switching on a telly and playing them an advert he has made to sell himself. Showing Harvey doing household chores, playing chess and looking after the kids, the pay-off line is: 'Every home needs a Harvey.'

Accompanied by the soundtrack of Bachman-Turner Overdrive's 1974 classic 'You Ain't Seen Nothing Yet', this ad might not have made us all rush out to buy TV advertising campaigns, but it certainly made us all fall in love with this tremendously talented woofer.

Top of the Pups

When he recorded the Beatles' track 'A Day in the Life', Paul McCartney added an ultrasonic whistle, audible only to dogs, at the very end. This was purely for the pleasure of his Shetland sheepdog.

A Glossy Coat

The mascot for Dulux paint, the Old English sheepdog breed that was adopted by the brand swiftly became universally known as a Dulux dog. First introduced in the 1960s, this hairy cutie has featured regularly in television adverts. Different dogs have starred in the adverts, but the very first paint pooch was Shepton Dash, who was the face of Dulux for eight years. Shep was succeeded by Fernville Lord Digby, who enjoyed star treatment, being chauffeured to the studio and benefiting from the expert training of celebrity dog trainer Barbara Woodhouse. He also had no less than three stunt doubles. Apart from Shepton Dash, all the Dulux dogs have been breed champions.

THE DOG LOVER'S DIGEST

Ohhh Yes

According to his website, the Churchill
dog, whose catchphrase is 'Oh yes', was
born under the sign of Gemini in 1996.
Listing his occupation as insurance guru
and his pet hates as flat-pack furniture, bad
drivers, cats and unfair insurance prices, the
nodding dog of the now famous advertising
campaign has been copiously cloned,
with toy versions available to purchase.

Sigmund, Smoking, Snogging and Song: Four Favourite Furry Ads

Henry the bloodhound appeared alongside the late Sir Clement Freud, grandson of Sigmund Freud, in a campaign for Chunky Meat dog food. Cast because he shared the same melancholic expression as Sir Clement, Henry was played by several different dogs over the years.

Credited in the adverts as 'the patron saint of pipe smokers', the star of the St. Bruno pipe tobacco adverts was for many years a lovable St Bernard dog, who invariably showed up bearing a packet of the baccy for the desperate smoker who had run out.

Accompanied by the soundtrack 'Will You Still Love Me Tomorrow?', the Real Fire advert featured a bulldog, a cat and a mouse. The dog kissed the cat and the cat kissed the mouse, and the nation gave a collective 'aaaaah' every time the ad was screened.

The coolest pup in TV marketing, the VW Polo dog was seen sitting in the passenger seat, being driven by a beautiful woman, and belting out 'I'm a Man' by the Spencer Davis Group. And they call it a dog's life!

The Tail End:
Intelligent and
Loyal

The reason a dog has so many friends is that he wags his tail instead of his tongue.

Anonymous

In 2009 researchers discovered what many dog owners have long suspected: that dogs are just as smart as children.

Claiming that dogs are able to comprehend up to 250 words and gestures, as well as count up to five and perform simple mathematical calculations, these experts used tests that had been originally designed for kids. The results were conclusive – the average dog is a smart cookie.

Border collies and retrievers were rated among the most intelligent breeds, while terriers fell into the 'nice but dim' category.

Professor Stanley Coren, a leading expert on canine intelligence at the University of British Columbia, Vancouver, was at the helm of the project and confirmed that most dogs are as able linguistically as a two-year-old child, with some dogs even able to recognise the names of items it was asked to fetch and correctly retrieve them.

The Loyalty of the Big-hearted Akita

One breed that is especially loyal is the Akita. A fluffy hound that looks very like its wolfy forebears, the first mention of Akitas in Japanese literature dates back to AD 712. But it is the story of an Akita called Hachiko that has given the breed its reputation for loyalty.

In the 1920s Hachiko accompanied Professor Eisaburo Uyeno of Tokyo to the Shibuya train station, where he would see his master off to work at the Imperial University. Every evening Hachiko would return to the station to welcome Uyeno home. One day in 1925 Uyeno suffered a stroke at work and died, never returning to his loyal companion.

Given a new home, Hachiko was forever escaping and returning to the home of his beloved master. Eventually realising that Professor Uyeno wasn't going to be found at home, he went to the next most likely place: the station. Refusing to budge, many regular passengers realised that he was waiting in vain for his master. Profoundly moved by his vigil, they began to bring food for Hachiko.

News of his incredible loyalty spread far and wide. In 1934 sculptor Ando Teru saw his statue of Hachiko erected at the station, where by now Hachiko had been waiting for the Professor for almost ten years.

But during the decade in which he waited this most faithful of dogs developed health problems. On 8 March 1935, Hachiko died.

Mourned by his nation, Hachiko's bones were buried next to his master's grave. Sadly, as the Japanese were just getting involved in World War Two, and metal was a precious commodity, Hachiko's statue was melted in order to make arms. However, after the war a group of Hachiko fans had another commissioned. Erected in 1948, you can still see his memorial at Shibuya station today.

Touring Japan in 1937, Helen Keller was given an Akita, which she asked for having heard the story of Hachiko.

There is no faith which has never yet been broken except that of a truly faithful dog.

Konrad Lorenz

Near this spot are deposited the remains of one
who possessed Beauty without Vanity,
Strength without Insolence,
Courage without Ferocity,
and all the Virtues of Man,
without his Vices.
This Praise, which would be unmeaning
Flattery if inscribed over human
ashes is but a just tribute to the Memory
of Boatswain, a Dog.

🐾 **John Cam Hobhouse on Lord Byron's
Newfoundland dog, from 'Epitaph to a Dog'**

Barking Mad

The phrase 'dog days' is believed to relate to the Dog Star, Sirius, which rises with the sun in the summertime. Many ancients thought this hot summer weather was responsible for sending dogs mad.

Sirius

Dogs V Cats

- While a cat will ignore you if it suits, a dog will always hang onto your every word, looking up at you adoringly while he does so.

- When you're sad, a dog will sense your mood and do all he can to make you feel better; nudging you and licking your hand and generally reassuring you that he is there and that he loves you. A cat won't give two hoots how you feel, just so long as you put his food down on the dot of dinnertime.

- When you return from a long day at work a dog will welcome you with a frenzy of barking, licks and tail-wagging. A cat will show you its bum, before stalking off in disgust as if to say, 'What sort of time do you call this?'

- A dog will proudly fetch your slippers for you. A cat will deposit a dead rodent in your slippers and then slink off leaving you to dispose/resuscitate the poor creature.

- A dog will almost always appreciate the food you provide for him. A cat will almost always turn his nose up at the food you provide, as if you had just served him with something scraped from the bottom of your shoe.

The difference between cats and dogs? Dogs come when they are called, cats take a message and get back to you.

Anonymous

The great pleasure of a dog is that you may make a fool of yourself with him and not only will he not scold you, but he will make a fool of himself too.

Samuel Butler

I love my little cat, I do
With soft black silky hair
It comes with me each day to school
And sits upon the chair
When teacher says 'Why do you bring
That little pet of yours?'
I tell her that I bring my cat
Along with me because...

Daddy wouldn't buy me a bow-wow! bow wow!
Daddy wouldn't buy me a bow-wow! bow wow!
I've got a little cat
And I'm very fond of that
But I'd rather have a bow wow wow!

Joseph Tabrar, 'Daddy Wouldn't Buy Me a Bow Wow'

I love my dog because...

of their complete enthusiasm for life; they throw their hearts and tails into everything they do.

Paws For Thought

If it wasn't for dogs, some people would never go for a walk.

Emily Dickinson

*To sit with a dog on a hillside
on a glorious afternoon is
to be back in Eden...*

Milan Kundera

*To his dog, every man is
Napoleon; hence the constant
popularity of dogs.*

Aldous Huxley

*Money will buy you a pretty
good dog, but it won't
buy the wag of his tail.*

Henry Wheeler Shaw

*I am I because my little
dog knows me.*

Gertrude Stein

The more one gets to know of men, the more one values dogs.

Alphonse Toussenel

Old dogs, like old shoes, are comfortable. They might be a bit out of shape and a little worn around the edges, but they fit well.

Bonnie Wilcox

The reason dogs have so many friends is because they wag their tails instead of their tongues.

Anonymous

The pug is living proof that God has a sense of humour.

Margo Kaufman

*The most affectionate creature
in the world is a wet dog.*

Ambrose Bierce

Resources

Websites

Animal training for film and TV
www.rockwoodanimals.com

Crufts
www.crufts.org.uk

Dog-friendly pubs
www.doggiepubs.org.uk

Dog-friendly walks
www.visitwoods.org.uk

Holidays in the UK with your dog
www.dogpeople.co.uk

Publications

Coile, Caroline *The Dog Breed Bible* (2007, Barron's)

Dilger, Andrew *Dash: Bitch of the Year* (2011, Summersdale Publishers)

Edward, Olivia *The More I See of Men, the More I Love My Dog* (2002, Summersdale Publishers)

Fogle, Bruce *RSPCA New Complete Dog Training Manual* (2006, DK Publishing)

Fogle, Bruce *The New Encyclopaedia of the Dog* (2000, DK Publishing)

Hawkins, Barrie *Twenty Wagging Tales: Our Year of Rehoming Orphaned Dogs* (2009, Summersdale Publishers)

Holt, Ben *Dog Heroes: True Stories of Canine Courage* (2009, Summersdale Publishers)

Jenkins, Garry *A Home of Their Own: The Heart-warming 150-year History of Battersea Dogs & Cats Home* (2010, Bantam Press)

Webster, Richard *Is Your Pet Psychic?: Developing Psychic Communication with Your Pet* (2002, Llewellyn Publications)

Organisations

Battersea Dogs & Cats Home
www.battersea.org.uk

Canine Partners
www.caninepartners.co.uk

Dogs Trust
www.dogstrust.org.uk

German Shepherd Dog Rescue
www.germanshepherdrescue.co.uk

The Guild of Dog Trainers
www.godt.org.uk

The Kennel Club
www.the-kennel-club.org.uk

Medical Detection Dogs
www.medicaldetectiondogs.org.uk

Medivet Animal Trust
www.ma-trust.org

People's Dispensary for Sick Animals (PDSA)
www.pdsa.org.uk

Retired Greyhound Trust
www.retiredgreyhounds.co.uk

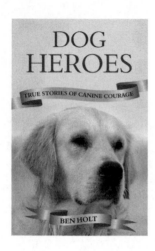

DOG HEROES

Ben Holt

ISBN: 978-1-84024-767-1

£7.99

Paperback

- Swansea Jack, the Labrador that rescued 27 people from drowning

- Max, the collie cross that warned his owner that she had breast cancer

- Shadow, the Rottweiler that saved three young children from a pair of hungry wolves

These are just a few of the inspiring true stories in this collection of dog tales from around the world. Included are some astonishing first-hand accounts by people who have witnessed quick-thinking and resourceful dogs in action.

From trained lifeguard dogs and guide dogs to loyal family pets and unnamed strays, each of these courageous canines has shown true heroism – sometimes in the most surprising of ways. Heart-melting, dramatic and often deeply moving, *Dog Heroes* proves why dogs can save and change lives, and are truly our best friends.

THE DOG
Ella Earle

ISBN: 978-1-84953-143-6

£6.99

Hardback

Combining gorgeous and characterful photographs with witty and heart-warming quotations, this enchanting celebration of our canine friends is a must-have for any dog lover.

Histories are more full of examples of the fidelity of dogs than of friends.

Alexander Pope

If you're interested in finding out more about our books, find us on Facebook at **Summersdale Publishers** and follow us on Twitter at **@ Summersdale**.

www.summersdale.com